Father Lucky

TRUST IN JESUS

The Remarkable Stories of a Priest, His Passions,
and the People Who Moved Him

**Father Clement Arthur Davenport,
"Father D"**

United States Army Colonel, Retired

Collected by Father Dariusz Iwański

Collected by: Father Dariusz Iwański

Editors: Charlotte Pace, Rosemary Alva

Transcription: Virginia Noh, Becky Ota

Cover design: Kelly Connelly

Production: Rosemary Alva

Special thanks to Yvete Barroso, John Conway, Bonnie Neylan,
Joe and Adele Personeni, Bunny Smith, Emily Skogstrom,
and Molly Widmer.

.   .   .   .   .

Nativity Series II

Menlo Park, CA 2011

We all need God.

Contents

Forward

In these past five years, it has been my great pleasure to come to know Fr. Davenport as he has come back to live at Nativity as pastor emeritus. I certainly knew of him from the many contacts I had with the parish when I was in the seminary. He has always enjoyed a sterling reputation as a fine priest and wonderful human being. In these last few years, I have come to see how genuine that reputation is.

I have heard his captivating stories of service as a chaplain in the United States Army, the happy years of his pastorate here at Nativity, the many stories about Fr. McKeon and Fr. Ford and, of course, his association with the 49ers. I have had the joy of playing a few rounds of golf with him (I am still waiting to beat him!) and of enjoying the many social occasions with parishioners.

My greatest memory will, however, be our trip to Lourdes in 2006. After raising the possibility of going on the pilgrimage with the Knights of Malta, his first question to me was, "Can I hear confessions there?" He did. Now he speaks about it as the greatest moment in his priesthood. In many ways, it combines what he loves about the priesthood, and his love for our Blessed Mother.

These characteristics are transparently obvious to anyone who comes to know him: his love of the Mass, of healing broken consciences in the Sacrament of Confession, of fidelity to Our Lady and service to God's people.

It is hard to imagine how many lives he has touched in his sixty years of priestly ministry. But a priest's fruitfulness is not measured in quantities, although, this alone is formidable in his case. I can say he has deeply touched my life by his shining example of selfless ministry. These stories help to capture a few samples of how he has touched the lives of others.

Ad multos annos!

Monsignor Steven D. Otellini

Chapter 1

My Family and Childhood

Mom's Conversion and Priesthood by Osmosis

My mother and father grew up in Palo Alto, right down here. The house where my mother grew up is on Lytton and Middlefield, and to this day every time I pass the house I think to myself, "That's where my mother grew up." Her mother, my grandmother, played the organ in the Baptist church; they were very, very anti-Catholic. But my mother used to walk down to St. Thomas Aquinas and she would go into the church because she loved the stained glass windows.

Later, she ended up meeting my father, who was Catholic, and they got married. But Dad would go/not go to church. Still, my mother promised that she would have the children baptized Catholic. So, one day in 1924 when she was pregnant with me, she went up to St. Joseph's Church in Berkeley and she walked around the block four times before she got the nerve to ring the doorbell. Finally, she rang the doorbell, and an Irish priest—I don't remember now who he was—opened the door. She told him, "I'm not a Catholic, but I

want to find out what you guys believe."
She was scared stiff. But she took
instructions from that priest, while
carrying me, and she was baptized three
weeks before I was born. And she used to
say to me, "The reason you're a priest is
because of osmosis."

Later, when I was at St. Patrick's, I
remember going home for lunch to my
grandmother's. When I entered the house
wearing the collar for the first time, it
was a shock to her. She was just a
typical Protestant little lady who was a
good person. She just wasn't sure about
the Church.

The Fighting Young Davenports

One of the first things I remember about
my childhood was fighting with my big
brother, William. He was two years older
than I and we used to have our fights.
But this one time, I think I was 8 years
old, I can distinctly remember. We had a
door with glass panes, and my brother was
outside and he was going like this to me,
and I went "Wham!" and I hit him through
the door. My brother's nose was all blood
coming out. My dad ran out, and first he
looked at my arm to see if I was cut. And
when he saw I wasn't cut, then he beat
the hell out of me.

William was my older brother. He served
in the Second World War. My younger
brother, Walter, was in Korea the same
time I was. He was with the 7th Division

With my parents, Tommy and Mina Davenport, at the Pacific Freight Station on Shattuck Avenue, Berkeley. I am on the left. My full name is Clement Arthur, but my maternal grandfather didn't like "Clement", so he started calling me "Art", which was also his name.

and I was with the 1st Division. We
didn't have a chance to communicate. He
was only there about a week and then he
went home. They rotated him. He had
enough points to rotate home.

The Depression
We went to elementary school at St.
Joseph's in Berkeley. I remember my First
Holy Communion. My mother was very, very
sick, carrying my younger brother, and
she couldn't come. I was wearing the
first suit I had with long pants. As I
ran home, I tripped and fell—and tore a
big hole in my pants. My mother took one
look at me and started to cry because
here I was, and they probably went out
and spent $10 to buy a suit. This was
around 1931 or 32, and so that was
expensive then, and here I was with a big
hole in the knee.

This was all during the Depression. My
dad was a postman. Then he became the
superintendent of the Richmond post
office. My mother said they cut the
salary but we still had steady income
coming in. I can see them sitting at that
table right now writing out a budget—this
much for this, and this, and this. To the
church, $1.00—that was all they could
afford—but that's what built those
churches. They also put aside ten cents
each for the kids so that we could see a
movie Saturday afternoon. It was ten
cents to see a movie. They had to work

Here I am pictured (right) with my older brother, William (left).

that into their budget. And I would sneak
my little brother in and then take his
money and buy candy. My younger brother,
Walter, was a nice little kid. We really
got along nicely. He is still alive. And
I still go over there for Christmas and
Easter.

.   .   .

The Cummins and the Davenports were
friends, and the Cummins family lived
just a couple blocks from us. Their boys
(Ben and Johnny) were younger, but we
walked together to school and also with
our parents to Sunday Mass at St.
Augustine's [Oakland]. Our parents always
prayed on the way to Church and we kids
were involved. At home we always prayed
the rosary every day before dinner. And
of course we had to say our prayers
before going to bed. I remember my mother
yelling, "Now Artie, did you say your
prayers?" And I'd cross myself and pray.
I was the first to enter the minor
seminary, followed by Ben and then
Johnny. Ben became a Monsignor and Johnny
became Bishop Cummins. I also became a
priest. So you see what happens when
the parents pray with their children.
It's one of the best things they can do
for them.

.   .   .

We had a pastor at St. Joseph's named
Father Thomas Brennan and he had four
homburg hats, you know those black hats?

And, every Saturday he asked me to go out and find his hats and he gave me 25 cents for every hat I found. One would be in the attic, one would be up in the belfry of the tower, one might be in the wine room, one might be in the workroom. And then I would get a dollar. I remember that very distinctly. And, then I would work for him in the summertime. I would paint the desks and paint the windows and stuff. He always used to say, "You'll be a good pastor because you can paint."

Father Brennan was one of those great priests. I thought at the time he was 100 years old, but he was probably younger than I am now.

When I was an eighth grader, Father Brennan said Mass over in the convent for the nuns at 6:45 a.m. I served that Mass every day for him. He wanted me to serve— that was pretty good. So every day, I walked about ten blocks to get up there, serve Mass, walk home for breakfast and walk back to start school. Yeah, Mass was at 6:45! That was for the nuns in the convent. In those days, of course, you had to learn the Latin.

.   .   .

I was just a little eighth-grade kid and you know how it is. There was a girls' school across the street and you weren't supposed to cross over to it, but I would always sneak across the street to see the girls. I would hear, "Now, now, you're not going to graduate." The pastor, Father Tom, loved me and he said, "Don't worry, you will pass and you will graduate." He made sure that I got the diploma. But Sister Thompson would say, "No, no. He's a bad boy." You know kids. What are you going to do?

Chapter 2

Vocation and Seminary

Getting Out of Class

When I was in the eighth grade at St. Joseph's in Berkeley, Father Harry Leonard had the job of vocation director. He went around to all of the schools and talked about the priesthood. If you were interested you would go down to Oakland for a day and take a test. And so I leaned over to the kid next to me—this was Todd Creed, who later became the announcer at Golden Gate Field, the horse races—and I said, "Todd, let's take the test and then we can get out of school for the day." And so we did. We went down to Oakland and took the test and I didn't think anything more of it.

Getting into St. Joseph's

One day in the summertime, I came home and my mother was sitting there crying and she said, "You passed." I said, "Passed what?" She said, "You took the test to go to the seminary and you passed. They came here, and we can't afford to pay. What are we going to do?" This was 1937, and financially it was still the Depression years, so the big thing was how they could finance me going. But then you could take out an insurance policy with the diocese and when you came through you paid the diocese back, which I did after 20 years.

I wasn't seriously thinking about the priesthood then. At 13, you don't really think maybe you could. I just wanted to get out of class. But I ended up going to the seminary. Seventy-nine of us showed up and of the seventy-nine of us who showed up, nine of us were later ordained. We went to the minor seminary at St. Joseph's College in Mountain View for high school and two years of theology. It gradually came on to me that this was really important, that I felt I was being called to the priesthood.

. . .

My favorite subject was English. Father John O'Neil was the instructor. I always got praise. I could write all kinds of things. I loved to write stories. I could write novels. I loved the seminary, both St. Joe's College and St. Patrick's. Although the main thing is, we were just kids running around playing football and basketball, making noise.

World War II
I remember when the war broke out. We were at St. Joseph's, and the president came on and announced that Pearl Harbor had been bombed, and that was the start of the war, 1941. About two weeks later,

he came back in and said that the poetry
class would no longer be here next year.
We would skip one whole year and go right
over to St. Patrick's Seminary. I guess
they wanted us to go right over to St.
Patrick's figuring we wouldn't get
drafted.

Blackouts
Every now and then the sirens would go
off at St. Patrick's for blackouts. I
guess someone spotted an unidentified
airplane or something. You stayed in your
room, and you turned out the lights and
everything. Then the siren would go on
again a little later, and you could turn
on your lights. There was rubber
conservation and gas rationing and there
were meat coupons. You had to take your
coupon book to the seminary office and
they would take the coupons out for the
summer vacation. My little brother was
growing up, and I think there was some
kind of coupon that you had to have for
shoes, and here was that little guy
growing up and needing new shoes every
six months.

The war wasn't necessarily worse than the
Depression. During the war people were
working, especially in the City.
Shipyards were open and people were
working building ships. And then in the
seminary I think I ate better than I did
as a kid at home. During the Depression
years there were a lot of beans. But at
the seminary the nuns would cook for us,

and you know we were grown by that time.

Father Mulligan
One day at St. Patrick's, someone knocked on my door. Father Mulligan, the president, was standing there. He asked, "Would you take a job as sacristan?" Which is kind of a good thing. And I said, "Oh yes, Father, I'll be glad to," right then. He said, "Now, may I make some suggestions?" And he started to poke me and he said, "I hear about you. You're around in the field always running around and yelling," and he kept poking me all the way back to my room, and I turned around and he left.

.   .   .

Both of my brothers were drafted. My older brother Bill was over in the South Pacific for four years. I'll never forget when he came back. Usually when a seminarian's brother would come back from overseas, you could go off for two weeks or so with your family. My brother was the first to come back, so I went up and knocked on the door to Father Mulligan and he said, "Yeah, what do you want?" And I said, "Father, I have great news, my brother just returned from the South Pacific after four years of being over there." And he said, "Oh, that's very nice, that's very nice, what do you want?" I said, "I would like to go home and see him." And he said, "Well, you tell him to come down and see you." And I said, "But he doesn't have a car." And he said, "Well, do you?" That was it. I went out and that was the end of it. That was Father Mulligan.

Nottum Knowum Latinum
I may have been good in English, but at first I was not very good in Latin, which was a problem, because at that time all of our classes at St. Patrick's were in Latin, and at first I didn't understand much of anything. So we come to this final test, and I ended up writing, "*Meum nottum knowum muchum Latinum.*" And the Professor, Father Wagner, sent back a note saying, "*Youum flunkum.*"

Seminary Summers and the REAL Reason the Jeep Went into the River
This was during vacation time when you're seminarians. Father Charlie Phillips had a camp for underprivileged kids from East/West Oakland, so we seminarians would go up as counselors. But this one year, I think I was in second year of high school, about 17 or 18, he had bought a brand new Jeep. He got us all together and he said, "Now this is a new Jeep we're using. I don't want any of you to wreck my Jeep!" So, about the second night we were there, I said I had to go into town for something. Marie, one of the other little counselors was there, and I said, "Marie, would you like to go into town with me?" She said, "Oh yeah." So she comes and jumps in the Jeep. So we're going down into town, and then I go

like this to put my arm around her—I was a seminarian—and we run right into the damn Russian River! I'm not kidding! So we had to stop because we're in the damn river, and we had to get a tow truck to pull us out! So I got back to camp and, geez, I tried to dry it out, but you know you could see it was all full of sand and stuff. And Father Phillips said, "What happened? What happened?" I said, "Well, Father, there was a squirrel running across the road and I tried to miss it, and I hit the river!"

Marie wrote me a letter in the seminary saying, "I know you are studying to be a priest, and I just want to let you know that if you ever decide to leave, I'll be here."

Me as a seminarian at St. Patrick's Seminary in Menlo Park, California.

Chapter 3

Ordination and Military Chaplaincy

I was ordained in 1948 and my first
assignment was at Holy Name in San
Francisco. Tom Bowe was the chancellor of
the archdiocese and he came there one
night and he said, "Art, do you like it
here?" I had just been ordained and I was
coaching football and running with the
kids and I said, "Yeah, I love it here."
And he said, "Well, Archbishop Mitty was
talking about sending you back to
Catholic U. for canon law." And with
Mitty it was never a question, like,
"I'll think about it," or "Could I get
back to you?" You went.

Tom Bowe said, "There's an opening at the
Presidio for a reserve chaplain and they
want a Catholic priest. So if you get
yourself into that he'll leave you
alone." So I said, "Well, how do I do
that? I haven't been ordained long
enough. I think you're supposed to be in
five years or so." But he got all the
paperwork done and so I got signed up. I
got my uniform and thought, "Wow. Now
I'll stick around Holy Name for awhile."

Call May Spiegel

One day I came home from my day off and there was a note on the board and I'll never forget it. It said, "Call Maj. Spiegel." I thought it said, "Call May Spiegel." So I called and the answer was, "Major Spiegel speaking." And I said, "This is Father Davenport." And he said, "Oh, congratulations, Father Davenport, you're in." And I said, "In what?" And, he said, "In the Army. You're in the Korean War."

December 18, 1948: My ordination in St. Mary's Cathedral, San Francisco, with Archbishop Mitty. I am kneeling, third from the left.

Chapter 4

The Korean War

Fort Huachuca and Barracks

So, here I am. I didn't do anything, but
now I have to go to a place where you get
shot at. But, God takes care of us. So I
went from Holy Name to Fort Huachuca,
Arizona. I lived in the barracks with 17
young lieutenants. But we each had a
room. I didn't have to do any drilling or
shoot a gun or anything.

Being in the military, you're a parish
priest. You baptize, you anoint, you hear
confessions, give them Communion, give
them instruction, take care of them, put
them to bed when they're drunk. I did
that a lot of times, too, you know,
especially at Fort Huachuca. I was in the
barracks with 17 second lieutenants, and
I was first lieutenant, and they're young
kids, away from home. It was fun.

Generals in Confession Lines

Not everyone can be in the position where
you're counseling superior officers. That
took some guts. Well, if you're an
officer and you come in the line to
confession, you're just like everyone

else. But one time this general came and I said, "You can come ahead," and he said, "Oh no, I'll wait in line like everyone else." And he was in line with a bunch of GIs for confession. He came in and went to confession just like everyone else. He said, "I'm a general but I'm also a sinner and I want to go to confession."

Strange Neighbors

The fort had a little hospital with four nurses there. Three were Catholics, and I remember this one, Annie. She was such a doll. One Saturday there was a knock on my door. It was the colonel and he says, "Father, I have a little nurse outside who wants to talk to you." So I went down, and Annie was there waiting. She had driven up in a little convertible and she had on some little shorts and a halter and she says, "Father, I've got some beer and sandwiches. Let's go down and have a picnic." And, I said, "I can't go out on a picnic with you." And she said, "Why not?" And I said, "In five minutes I would be all over you!" So off she goes in a huff and I said to myself, "You're such a dummy. Why didn't you go?" Later there's a knock on the door and it's the colonel standing there again, and he says, "Father, I'm a married man. I have a wife and four kids, and I heard everything that went on down there, and if she had asked me I would have gone in a minute."

The worst situation I had there was when the little wife of a Protestant minister came to me. They were both young and he went off to chaplain school. The senior chaplain at the fort would go over to her house at nighttime, knock on her door, and want to visit with her. He wanted to do more than visit with her. She came to me and she said, "Father, I am terrified." I said, "What's wrong?" She said, "Well, this chaplain comes over and keeps making advances to me. I am all alone in this place." I said, "Well, you just let me handle it." So I called him in. I think he was a lieutenant colonel. He was superior to me. I said, "Chaplain, I'm only going to say this once. I don't want to hear this minister's wife have any more complaints about you." He looked at me and said, "What do you mean?" I said, "You know what I mean." I said, "You are NOT to go over and bother her anymore. If you do, she's gonna tell me and I'm going to report you to the Colonel." He never went to her house again.

. . .

The fort was outside Bisbee, Arizona, about 40 miles east of Tucson. It's a little mining town. I went into town the first week I was there to introduce myself to the pastor because I was assigned to him as his assistant for marriage problems and so forth. I knocked on the door. He opened it and said,

"Yes?" And, I said, "I'm the priest from Fort Huachuca. I'm a new priest here and I've been assigned to be your assistant for marriage and so forth." And he said, "Is there anything I can do for you?" And I said, "No, but I figured, let's go have a drink." And he said, "Okay," and slammed the door. And then the little bugger called me and he said, "Special collections. Couldn't you have some special collections for my parish?" But at least the guy could have invited me in for dinner.

On to Korea

The whole reserve at Fort Huachuca was sent to Sacramento. Everyone except me. I wound up in Korea. I enjoyed it. Well, didn't enjoy it, but it was great priest work, anointing these kids and they're scared.

The Troop Ship and All-Night Confessional

I remember going on the troop ship to Pusan. We had about 3,000 soldiers on that ship. I got on the first day, as a priest, and I said, "Now I'm in such-and-such stateroom, if anyone wants to go to confession." I figured a few kids would want to come. Well, I went for 36 hours straight hearing confessions. The guys would come in and get me for chow and I would go eat and go pee and then go back to hear more. These kids were scared. They were going to war.

The Freezing North

We got off and there was a train that had come in. We were getting on the train to go to the front and these other kids were getting off the train and rotating home. The train was waiting on the tracks, and there was this kid looking at me and he says, "You're going to freeze your ass." He was right. It was cold. You don't realize how far north Korea is. We were way up north. It felt like Siberia. The wind blows 30 below, and geez it's cold. I got the flu, and I was really, really sick. I went to the medics and I had a 106-degree temperature. So they gave me some pills and said, "You'll get over it."

.   .   .

In some places we would make makeshift chapels out of sticks, just to get some cover from the cold. It would be 30 below. You'd have a pair of long johns and you'd have two pairs of pants. Then you'd have to have your flak jacket. It was just unbelievably cold.

The Password

I got my orders there to go the 45th Division—Oklahoma Division. I'd be with a regiment. I got up there, and the first night I was so tired I didn't even get the password. So I climbed to bed in my little bunk and went sound to sleep. In the middle of the night I had to go to the john. I didn't know where to go, so I got up and I went up where some kids were standing. The guard said, "Halt, who goes there? The password!" And I will never forget. The guard's first word was "Golden!" And I was supposed to say, "Bear." That was the password—but I didn't know that it was. And I said, "Well, I am a priest, I just got in…." The kid standing guard said "Father, you better learn the password." The kid was more scared than I was, but I will never forget that the first night the password was "Golden Bear."

The Chinese Onslaught

We were with the 45th Division, the Oklahoma Division. I was with the infantry. In chaplain school they didn't tell you anything. We never heard a shot. But my first time in Korea, the officers would say, "Hey, Father, we want you to cover such and such." You have to make sure you set things up for the men. We had about seven chaplains. I was the regimental chaplain. We had two South Korean divisions on either side of us and we were in the middle. The Koreans weren't well trained, and the Chinese would come around through their side and get us from the back.

The "Suez Canal"

The Chinese, you could hear them. There were thousands, and here we were with these two Korean divisions on either side of us, paper thin. The Chinese were just unbelievable. I remember one night being out there and they started approaching. We went about three hours, and they just kept coming up and coming up and we were machine-gunning them and so forth. Finally, around maybe 5:00 in the morning, the commanding officer came up to me and said, "Father, how many bodies do you think we have out there?" I had no idea. And he said, "We figure it must be at least 3,000 right in front of us." Young kids, young Chinese kids. We captured some of them and they thought they were fighting in the Suez Canal. They had no idea what they were doing.

The Marines Save the Day

So the Communists would come in behind us and that was no fun. But we always got out of it. One time we were about to be overrun, and the Seventh Marine Division— a great outfit—was right next to us and they came around and saved our necks. It's nice to have the Marines. They're a proud outfit. They are because they had one rifleman and nine cameramen. Well, that's what I kept saying to them, "You guys have one rifleman and nine cameramen." The Marines are good.

Moral Issues

As a chaplain you're always dealing with kids with horrible moral problems, with killing the enemy. A lot of them were worried about killing, which is good because they don't want to kill anybody. But they were there, and they had to. And then you had to talk to the kids who didn't want to go out, and you had to talk to them about not going to the brig, and they were scared.

Cord Rosaries
And one thing that would help me was the cord rosaries. You know, people make them by hand. Well, there was something I did one time and it ended up in the *New York Times*, a story about this young priest in the Korean War. And about two weeks later, I got a letter from a lady in a wheelchair who said she read about me in the *New York Times*. She said she makes cord rosaries and she asked if I could use any cord rosaries, and I said, "Yeah." So I get a box full of hundreds of these rosaries, and I would pass out these rosaries, and put them around the kids' necks. They would go out on patrol and the rosaries didn't make any noise or anything. And all the black kids wanted the rosaries. They would have a rabbit's foot and a rosary.

A Special Holy Communion
But let me tell you the best thing that happened to me, and it's a good lesson. I had this Col. Clemmons. He wasn't even Catholic, but he was a pretty religious guy. We were up in the trench war in Korea and we knew we were going to be attacked that night. I had the Blessed Sacrament with me and was hearing kids' confessions. Col. Clemmons comes up and says, "I want to receive Holy Communion, Father." And I said, "Sorry, sir, you're

not Catholic. The Protestants are having services down in the rear area down there." And he says, "No, no, Father, if I go down there, they're going to preach and sing hymns. I want to receive God." I said, "Well, sir, do you really believe that this is the Body and Blood of Jesus Christ?" And he said, "Yeah, Father, I really do." And I said, "Okay, Colonel, I will give you Holy Communion but you've got to promise me that you're going to do something about this." And he said, "Okay, Father, I will." And so he knelt down and I gave him Holy Communion. And he got wounded that night and they took him back to Tokyo Army General, so I don't know what happened to him. I asked the bishop from the Navy about my giving the colonel Holy Communion, and he said, "You were perfectly right to do that." But I always wouldn't worry in wartime. It was a great lesson for me, for this man to kneel down and say, "I want to receive God."

Two Stories of Finding the Faith
One day we were out there in the trenches, and word got out that we were about to be hit by the Chinese. A soldier came to me and said, "Father, I wasn't baptized, and I want to receive Our Lord in Holy Communion and I know all this and I believe all this stuff." So I said, "Okay." I took my canteen and I baptized him and gave him Holy Communion, and I said, "I'll see you next week." And then this big fight broke out and I don't know

what happened, but I didn't see him
again, or find out whether he got home.
Five or six years later, I was saying
5:00 Mass at Nativity, and afterward
there was this guy standing in the
sacristy with two little babies in his
arms and he says, "Are you Father
Davenport and were you a chaplain in the
Army with the 45th Division?" And I said,
"Yes." He said, "Do you remember
baptizing me in the trench?" He was
visiting someone in the area and he
attended the 5:00 Mass with his two
little daughters he was carrying and he
said, "I recognized you by your voice."
What a wonderful thing. I never knew. I
baptized this kid, gave him Holy
Communion, and then heard nothing. A
happy ending.

Another time I had a lieutenant colonel
who was my boss and he was a Presbyterian
or something. And I would say Mass every
afternoon, and I would look up and always
see him in the back pew. So finally,
after a few weeks, when he came in I said
to him, "Chaplain, I would like to talk
to you." He came around and I said to
him, "Sir, I see you here every day. Are
you coming here to check up on me or
what?" He said, "No, no, Father. I
believe in the Real Presence and my
church doesn't." So we got to talking and
he was a lieutenant colonel about ready
to retire, another year left in the
service. He was married and had four
kids. So I wrote a letter of introduction

for him to Bishop Manning. When he
retired, Bishop Manning gave him and his
wife instructions and baptized them, so
he and his whole family were brought into
the Church. He couldn't do it beforehand
because he would have lost his pension
and everything else.

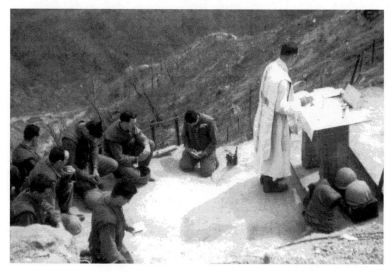

Offering Mass in Korea.

Mass in Korea. In both of these photos you can see our makeshift chapels.

Walter Cronkite's Unfair Report

Walter Cronkite was down with his camera crew. Our kids were going out on patrol looking for rockets because the Communists were rocketing the city. So Cronkite went to this one little GI and he said, "Are you a member of the First Division?" The GI said, "Yes sir!" Cronkite said, "What are you looking for?" And the kid said, "Rockets." Cronkite said, "What does a rocket look like?" And the kid said, "I don't know!" Well he never saw a rocket! So that night on the news, Walter Cronkite says, "First Division troops are wandering around in the jungle not knowing what they're doing." Very unfair.

A Real M.A.S.H. Unit

You guys have seen "M.A.S.H." The priest there is kind of a buffoon, but if you watch that for a while you see that he has some pretty good moments. I used to go once a week to this M.A.S.H. hospital and I would put on my stole. There were a lot of Koreans, and most of the time they didn't know what a stole meant. But every once in awhile some Koreans would recognize that stole and get all excited because they would know that I was a priest and they could get Holy Communion and be anointed. So that was a good memory. Wearing just a simple stole would indicate that I was a priest.

But also, every Saturday night or so, I would go to the M.A.S.H. and pick up two different nurses and bring them back to our HQ where there was a little tent set up with a bar and they could dance. And these kids could dance with them and smell their perfume. And the girls loved it. They put on their lipstick, and for them it was great. I would leave them alone, and then around midnight I would come back and say, "Okay, girls. It's past your bedtime. We have to go home." And everyone would boo me.

Those nurses were terrific. The doctors would patch you up, but the nurses would heal you.

Burning Tanks

The kids in the hospital. I can't imagine myself looking down and not having a leg. Or not having a face. A lot of them get burned. The kids in the tanks. The nurses called them "crispy critters" because the tanks were so incendiary and had the tendency to burn up. The kids couldn't get out. And they had these anti-tank guns that would go through almost anything, and it ricochets, and all those kids would be killed.

Calls for Mother

I talked to another priest quite often about how a kid who was dying would call for his mother. Never for a father, always call for their mother. It's not that they don't love their fathers, it's just a difference. It's just their first instinct. That's traumatic when you're holding a kid in your arms who is calling out for his mommy. Miserable. And now I say it's the same thing, in this world of ours that's going all to hell, and it's Mary that we're calling for. When you're in real danger, it's Mother that you think of. I think we go back to the womb or something.

One time in particular I remember, we were in the trenches and I would go up and say Mass for the different companies. This one kid wanted to be a baseball player, and every time I went to his company he had two mitts and a ball, and he made me play catch with him. We're in the trenches throwing the ball back and forth. And everyone would be looking at us. And he insisted on serving my Mass. He would say, "Father, I'm serving your Mass." He was a kid from the South, black kid, good kid. About a week later we got attacked by the Chinese, and they came pouring through, BOOM BOOM. He got hit in the neck. And I got hold of him and got this other guy and we carried him down to the aid station. They got him on the stretcher and the doctor looked at me and shook his head. Evidently the shell severed his artery, and blood was spurting everywhere. And he was just yelling, "Mama! Mama!" and he died. As I said, it's comparable to our world which is morally and spiritually dying and we need our Blessed Mother and we should pray out to her, "Mama, Mama."

The Ultimate Ethical Question

One time, after an attack, we were hit heavy and all the officers were dead. The CO comes in a helicopter and says, "You are going to be surrounded, and it looks like you're probably going to be captured." And he says to me, "There is no officer alive. I would like you to stay with the men even though you're going to be captured because at least you know what to do." He says, "You don't have to do this, but if you're gonna leave, you've got to come with me because we gotta get out of here right now!" I said, "No, I'll stay." At that moment the sergeant threw me his M-1, his rifle. I said, "I don't need this, I'm a noncombatant." He says, "No, you may need it."

I had 17 wounded kids there. There were dead kids too. And he had said, "Father, we can't stop them from coming through." But as a priest, I was thinking about how I was holding this gun, and there were kids here. I thought, "Geez, I'm not supposed to be shooting anybody and killing them. I'm a priest. Would it be wrong for me to shoot, say a Korean, or whatever they might be, or could I stand by and let them stab a wounded kid?"

It never came to the point where they got through the wire. The helicopters came in with rockets and they kept the Communists from coming through. But it always bothered me as a priest. I remember going

to the auxiliary bishop in the military
ordinariate, a nice man, and I said to
him that it's always bothered me as a
priest in the service, and I explained it
to him and said, "Morally, Bishop, would
I have been wrong to kill somebody?" He
said, "No, no. You're defending life.
Therefore, you had all the right in the
world to kill anybody."

They would have come in and bayoneted the
kids, you know. But they didn't break
through.

Don't Call Him Chappy, Call Him Father Lucky

Everyone gets tired at times, and this
one day I was coming to the chow hall and
I was really down and tired. This young
lieutenant says, "Hi, Chappy, how are
ya?" and pokes me. Chappy, chaplain. Well
I said to him, "Whatever you want, don't
call me 'Chappy' and don't poke me," and
he said, "Oh, Chappy." So I hit him and
went WHAM, and down he goes. And I can
see him now. So I helped pick him up and
I'm thinking to myself, "I shouldn't have
hit him." Well, my commanding officer was
there and afterwards he said to me, "Gee,
you shouldn't have done that, but it was
the best thing I ever saw." But that
lieutenant never poked me again and never
called me "Chappy" again. It wasn't
right, but it served a purpose.

. . .

There were so many traumatic stories. There was one case where this kid was killed because he didn't get the password. It was his first time on a patrol, and he got lost and he turned around and came back. Another kid, just newly arrived, was on guard, and he asked, "Who's there?!" The other kid didn't know the password, so the kid on guard shot and killed him. I had to take care of the poor kid who shot him. It wasn't his fault.

. . .

Another time, some of these kids were coming back from R&R in Japan. I said to this one kid, "Come here and I'll hear your confession." And he said, "Oh no, Father. But the next time I see you I'll go." And I said, "Okay." I think to myself, what are you going to do? So two or three of them went this way and I went that way with another guy. Well about ten seconds later, WHOOSH. We ran back, and all those kids I had just been talking to were all blown up. It was a question of missing by just a few feet, that much difference. And someone called me "Father Lucky." And from then on the kids would say, "Oh, here's Father Lucky."

An Exhausting Day and Mass for Two
Danny Visconti was my driver, and he drove me everywhere. He was a nice kid from Brooklyn and he hadn't been going to Mass or church. And so I said to him,

"Danny, you're not going to miss Mass anymore." And he said, "Why not?" "Because you're going to be my driver." And he said, "Oh geez." We became good friends because you do everything together. You eat together and sleep together and everything else. Dan was just a typical kid. My big problem was that he used the F word a lot, and I tried to break him of that. But what ended up happening was that I started using the F word.

You have to understand that the roads are all mud and ice and you're going up these mountains to get to where our tanks are, and I tried to do it once a week to say Mass for the kids and give them Communion. But this one day, geez, it was cold and windy and we started out and the Jeep hit this bridge and got stuck half out of the water. I got out and said to Danny, "You stay here and watch the Jeep. Give me the 45 and you keep your rifle." So I'm walking along trying to find a truck or something to get us out of this river. And finally, I saw this deuce and a half (which is a big truck) and these Korean soldiers were chopping down the logs to make bunkers with. I came to the lieutenant in charge and tried to talk him into pulling us out. He says, "One, two, three, four o'clock." And I said "Now." And he said, "No. Four o'clock." So I took out the gun and I said, "Now!" And so he got in the truck and they pulled us out, and I gave them cigarettes and so forth and on we went. I wouldn't have shot him, you know that. But for a noncombatant I convinced him.

The whole thing went on all day long, and finally we got out to where the tanks were supposed to be. They were gone, and no one had told me. We were all cold and wet, and we got back and it was just about chow time. I told Danny, "I'm going to say Mass and then I'll fix something." And he said, "Father, I want to serve your Mass." So I said the Mass, just the two of us. When I finished, Danny tugged on my sleeve and said, "Father, it was really good serving your Mass today." And I said, "What do you mean?" And he said, "There was just something different about it." And all I can say is that I felt something at that Mass. I had been ordained and been to the cathedral for High Mass, and I never had the feeling of the presence of Christ as I did at that Mass. But what got me was that that's what I was feeling. But when Danny called me and said, "Hey Father, there was something different today." He felt the same thing. So I don't know, but my point is that I think that God gives you a little pat on the head when you're kinda down and discouraged and He wants you to know He's there with you.

The Kid Who Wasn't Afraid
Another time, there was a change in drivers, and I had this kid from Cincinnati as my driver, and it was the

first time he was on the front lines. He
was a big awkward kid who wasn't a very
good driver, but anyway there was a tank
that was stopped and we drove up and I
was talking to the kid driving the tank.
All of a sudden, these mortar rounds come
in. The Cincinnati kid hit the deck and—
BOOM—we were covered with dirt, and
shrapnel was hitting the Jeep, and we
were lying there, so I turned my head and
said, "Are you scared?" He said, "Not
when I'm with you, Father." I said, "Well
I am! Let's get the hell out of here!"
I'll never forget him, "Not when I'm with
you, Father."

God's Will
Did I ever tell you about the kid I
shared the same birthday with? Yeah,
August 19th. Well this kid was driving a
deuce-and-a-half, that's a big truck, a
big Army truck with six to eight wheels
in the back. I had just been up there
saying Mass for a company and I was
coming back down and there was this
deuce. So I stopped my Jeep and started
talking to the kid and he was all
excited. He said, "Geez, Father, it's my
birthday!" I think he said he was 19. I
said, "Well, that's great." And I said,
"Now be very careful going up. Make sure
you stagger your speed. Make it go fast
and slow so that they can't just watch
you and drop the rounds on you." So the
kid said, "Okay, Father." So off he
takes. Just a few seconds later, we hear
this big boom, and I said, "Danny, turn

around, let's go back up there." So we turn around and sure enough here is this big truck on its side and this kid is there all bloody, all shot up. I had time to anoint him. He said, "Father, am I dying?" and I said, "Yes," and he says, "Why?" And with that he died. By that time other GIs were around. There was this old lifer sergeant, you know with a cigarette out of the side of his mouth, and he said, "Father, tell 'im it was God's will." I said, "It was NOT God's will! God's will was this kid should have grown up, had his babies, had his family, lived a life, and then gone to heaven. It wasn't God's will that this kid should be blown up on a foreign land someplace!" Boy, that place was quiet as hell. This old sergeant came back later to the sacraments.

We All Need God

Another thing I think about are the flyers who used to come in when we'd get a stand-down. They used to fly me all over the place when I had to get somewhere. They would come in and want to go to town or someplace, not that they could do much. I had four Jeeps under my control because I had seven chaplains, and these flyers would say, "Hey, Father, how about borrowing your Jeep?" I'd say okay. So one time this kid came in—he wasn't a Catholic, I don't think he was, anyway—we were talking and he said, "You know, Father, I'm a lawyer, I've got a great job waiting for me, I've a beautiful wife and a wonderful little girl." He said, "I don't see that I have any need for God in my life." Well, gee, that kinda gave me the shivers, you know, oh gee.

Almost a week later he came by again and wanted to borrow a Jeep to go into town. I said okay, and he said, "Father, why don't you come in with me?" I said, "Okay, I haven't been into town in a long time. I can see the nuns." There was an orphanage there and I used to drop in on the nuns. So I went to get my helmet and my flak jacket and while I was doing that, the phone rang and it was the sergeant major saying that the colonel wanted to see me. So I said to the kid, I forget his name now, he was a lieutenant, "Gee, I can't go. I've got to go see the colonel. You go ahead." So I turn around and start walking to headquarters and he went on to the Jeep. And I'd say about 10 seconds or so later—BOOM—he hit a land mine. I was the first one to get to the Jeep, and of course he was all shot up. So, we flew him back to the hospital, and the next day I flew down to see him. I remember he had one arm all in a cast, and with his other arm he reached over to me and he said, "Father, can you teach me to find God?" I'll never forget that. The one week before, he had a life that was rosy and all this stuff. I don't know whatever happened to him. "I don't need God in my life." It gave me the shivers. We all need God.

The Morgue

I had a job to do that always bothered me. We had a morgue, and every night you would go in at 1:00 a.m. and see all these kids who died during the day. There would be a doctor there and he would zip open the bag and write what caused the death. And this one time there was this new doctor from New York, an Italian kid, and they told him, "Doctor, you have to go in tonight at one," and he was kind of sick thinking about it. And I said, "Don't worry, Doctor, I'll go in with you." And he said, "I appreciate that, Father."

And, several times, you open those bags and the blood would come out and it meant that the kid bled to death. The kids at the front thought that the kid was dead and so they put him in the bag.

I anointed all those kids. There were hundreds over the years. I gave absolution, Communion to the dying— hundreds. The problem is, there were so many times you see kids all shot up. You never see them again. You don't know if they live or if they die.

The Letters to Parents

And then I used to write to all the parents of these kids who had been killed. I would write to every one of them in our outfit that died. And you try so hard not to make it a standard letter. You hope that you can say something personal, that you met this kid or had seen him or something like that. The letters you get back, too, were unbelievable. You know, people have faith and say, "Thank God that there was a priest with him and he had the last rites." And they would ask if he suffered and you would say no. But you don't know whether they suffered.

The Real Meaning of War
It's stupidity. War is stupidity. No one ever wins war.

Chapter 5

Return from Korea

From Foe to Friend

Sometime after the war, I was at Camp
Roberts and I came in and saluted the
officer I was reporting to. The first
thing he said to me, before he even
returned the salute, "I don't like
Catholic priests." I said, "Okay sir, but
you're stuck with me." But I would say
that in a couple months' time we became
good friends.

Sneaking Out for Golf

I came back from Korea and went to St.
Bernard's in Oakland. The bishop said
they had a problem. The pastor was this
little Irish guy, Danny Kelly, who had
had a stroke. There was an administrator
there and he hated the place. And the
bishop asked me to go down there and kind
of settle things. When I arrived, I rang
the doorbell and Danny opened the door,
looked at me and said, "I don't like
priests who play golf." And, that's how I
was greeted. And I said, "Well, we're
going to get along real well together."
Which we did. Eventually.

On the first Friday I was there, I wanted to go out and play golf, and I wondered to myself: Okay, now I know this is going to be a problem. What do I do? Do I ask him? Do I sneak out? I decided to ask him. I put my golf clothes in the blue bag, put on my golf hat and collar, went down and knocked on his door and he looked at me. His eyes got real big and I said, "Father, I just want to let you know that I'm going to be gone for about four hours." So I went down and took off to play golf. And then every Friday there would be something and I would say, "Oh no, I can't because I have to play golf." And he never had a problem. When he later left, he said to me, "Art, I was waiting for you that first Friday and if you had snuck out I would have been all over you." By that time he had mellowed.

Last-Minute Last Rites

I got this call one day that a mother and daughter had had a fight and they wanted to know if I would come over. So I went over and found that the daughter had stabbed the mother. The daughter was a high school kid. Blood was all over, so I called the cops and the ambulance came. We got the mother down to the hospital and I anointed her. We had the girl in jail and I was helping her because she was distraught. She had blood all over her. Finally, after a couple of hours I go back to the rectory and there's a note on the stairs. It said, "Art, there is a sick call at such-and-such a house." So I grabbed my oils, went over there, and found the woman and anointed her. I had just ten seconds before she died. I anointed her and she was conscious and then she closed her eyes and died.

I went home and went straight to Danny and said, "You're a priest and I'm a priest. For hours today I was with a girl who stabbed her mother. You were sitting on your ass up here all day. There was a lady dying and you should have been there." I grabbed him and said, "If you ever do that again I'm going to beat the shit out of you." And he said, "Oh, Art, don't do that, don't do that." He would never do that again.

Chapter 6

St. Mary's Hospital

Talks with Archbishop Mitty
I stayed at St. Bernard's as assistant
about five years, I think, and almost ran
it. Then I got sent to St. Mary's
Hospital to be the chaplain there. That
was tough work.

Archbishop Mitty was there at the time.
He was in a room up there on the fifth
floor, same as me, right near the chapel.
One of my jobs was every afternoon I
would bring him Communion, of course, and
then every day I would take him upstairs
and walk him on the patio up on the top
of the hospital. We would talk about
different things. But this one day, I
came by and I opened the door to his room
and looked in, and he had these tears
coming out. I said, "Archbishop, what's
wrong?" He said, "Oh, I was just thinking
that when I die, all the priests are
gonna be happy." I said, "That's not
true!" Was he tough? Naww, he was a good
man. He was all for the Church—but he was
tough, yeah he was tough.

The Nun and the "Convert"

When you're chaplain, you go to everybody who comes into the hospital. You greet 'em, find out what their religion is, do they want to talk to a priest, and so forth. Well, this one fellow was a very nice man. He was a Lutheran, and I'll never forget him: a very holy man. I went to him, told him I was a Catholic priest and so forth, and asked him if there was anything I could do for him. He said, "No, Father." He says, "I love my faith, and what I am doing." I said, "I'll give you a blessing," and he said, "Thank you." I gave him a blessing and I left. Next day, one of the sisters came to me and said, "Father, Mister so-and-so, do you know him?" I said, "Yes, Sister!" She said, "He's dying to be received into the Church. Will you please go visit him?" I said, "Right now?" And I went right then and there and I walked in. He said, "Oh, hi, Father, how are ya?" I said, "Now look, this nun keeps telling me that you want to be received into the Church, that you want to be Catholic." He said, "No, Father, I am really happy with my own faith. I love Jesus and I hope that's good enough." I said, "God bless you. You're a good man. I know God will bless you and put His arms around you. I won't bother you anymore." Believe it or not, again she got me! She said, "Father, I just left him and he's saying, "Get the priest, I want to be baptized." I go down and walk in and I look at him and I say, "Now what's going on?" He said,

"Father, do anything to me, just get that
nun off my back!" He said, "Bless me,
give me Communion, whatever." I said,
"No, no, no. You just tell Sister the
next time she comes to you that I forbade
her to talk to you and she must talk to
me first." She came to me and I said,
"Look, you are disturbing him when he is
ready to die. Just leave him in peace."

Chapter 7

First Years at Nativity

I stayed at St. Mary's for about a year.
At that time, Leo Maher was secretary of
the bishop and he asked me, "Art, do you
like the work here?" And I said, "Sure,
but I find it very confining. I always
wanted to be a parish priest." And he
said, "Well, you do a good job and the
nuns like you." So I didn't think
anything more of it. But next thing I
knew, a letter came out assigning me here
as assistant pastor to Father McKeon.

Who Can't Hear Whom?
Father McKeon was a great old guy. At
that time, the church didn't have a
loudspeaker system. And so I kept saying,
"Father, we should really get a
loudspeaker system because when we preach
they can't hear us." And he would say,
"No." Finally, one day when I was going
on vacation, I saw an electrical
equipment truck here, and I asked them,
"What are you doing?" And they said,
"We're putting a loudspeaker system in
the church." I went back inside and said,
"Father, that's so great we're getting a
loudspeaker system." And he said, "Yeah,
the people were complaining that they

couldn't hear you." Well, you all know everyone can hear me clear to the back. People couldn't hear Father McKeon after the second row.

The Disappearance of Tina

I had this great little dog here at Nativity, a German Shepherd that our cook, Mrs. O'Brien, had got for me. I came home one day and there was this little puppy. I called her Tina. She would run up at recess and play with kids in the yard. Father McKeon even got to like that dog. He would go out to read in the front of the office, and the dog would come and lay her head on his foot.

In those days, Father Columban, a black priest who taught at Atchison, Kansas, would come out to Nativity every summer. And the people loved him. One summer I was going on vacation, and I told Father Columban, "Father, it's your job to take care of my little dog here." And he said, "Oh, I'll take care of her." While I was gone, they let the dog out at night to do her little things and then she would go back to my room to sleep. One night Father Columban put her out, and a short time later he heard a car go by. That dog would jump into any car. And he heard the car take off. The dog was never found again. George Potter was the police chief and when I got back he said, "Father, we've had a lot of dognapping. People take thoroughbred dogs and then they sell them." And my dog was a thoroughbred.

Really beautiful. But I never wanted to get attached to a dog again. It was real hard, you know.

Father McKeon's Anointing

I was here with Father McKeon for two years and then he died. I remember anointing him in that room right there. He had pneumonia. He didn't want to go to the hospital. And I said "Father, you've got to." And he said, "Well, if it makes you feel any better then go ahead and anoint me." That was about six months before Father Ford came.

Father Ford: The Priests' Priest

You had to know Father Ford. He was something else. He was a beautiful man. I remember standing right there, having a beer. It was July and a hot day, and Nativity had been six months without a pastor. I was drinking a beer with Claire Delaney, a nurse from Sequoia. There was a knock at the door and I opened it. I'm standing there with my beer, and Father Ford comes in and he says, "Who are you?" I said, "I'm an assistant here, Father Davenport. Who are you?" And he said, "I'm your new pastor, Father Ford. And who is she?" And I said, "Only a friend of mine." And he said, "Oh my God," and walked upstairs.

And so I walked up with him and showed him his room. Now Father McKeon—who was there before—was a wonderful old man but he had had books, and unsigned checks, and he had, oh, what a mess. And so before Father Ford came I had everything cleared out, and now there was nothing in the room but a ladder. And so I tell Father Ford, "This is your room." And he looks at me and then walks over to the ladder, climbs up on it and sits, and he says, "What have I got myself in for?"

Father Ford was a priest's priest. He was one of the greatest priests that ever lived. And a lot of priests would come to him and talk to him when they had problems.

Getting Kicked Out of Better Places

Years later, when I had to go to Fort Ord because of the war in Vietnam, Father Ford would come down to visit. He would come down and we would play golf and have dinner. And this one time he came down and he said, "Art, we're invited to a cocktail party by this Navy chaplain." It was Major Joe Clooney, who was very strict, and I was only a major. And I said, "Oh no. I know Joe. I won't be welcome. There will be admirals and stuff." And he said, "Oh, don't worry about it."

So we played 18 holes of golf and we go up to this place. And there are admirals and all this big fancy stuff. Sure enough, Joe Clooney comes over and says, "Art, you're not welcome here." And I say, "Joe, I don't want to be here. But Father Ford wants me to be here." So he says, "Well, get him out and tell him to leave." So I go to Father Ford and say, "Joe just said we need to leave." And he says, "Don't worry about it." Now there's this kid with a banjo and really long hair. Next thing we know, we're with the kid with the banjo, and Joe comes over and says, "Get him out of here!" So Father Ford turns around and says to everybody, "I've been kicked out of better places than this."

Chapter 8

Assignment to Vietnam

The Nonsmoker Grabs the Cigarettes

After a few years at Nativity, I got
assigned to St. Thomas the Apostle up on
Balboa in the City. One day in 1968, the
chancellor, Monsignor Thompson, came down
after work and said, "Hey, the archbishop
said he wants to see you tomorrow in his
office at 10:00." And I think, "Geez,
that's great. I'm getting a parish." So I
go down there at 10:00 and I go in and
Archbishop McGucken says, "Art, come on
in," and how are you and so forth. And he
says, "I want you to read this letter." I
read the letter and it's from Cardinal
Spellman about the need for new priests.
So I said, "Oh, I guess you want me to
recommend some young priests to go into
the Army." And he says, "Oh, no, they'll
never go. How about you?" I reached over
and grabbed his cigarettes—I had stopped
smoking—and I grabbed his cigarettes. And
he said, "Art, what's wrong?" And I said,
"Well, I thought you were giving me a
parish when you asked me over." And he
says, "Oh don't worry, Art, you'll get
that later."

So, I said "Sure," and two weeks later I was off to Fort Ord for some training. Then on to Vietnam.

Nine Sunday Masses

In Vietnam, I was brigade chaplain and I had seven ministers working for me and I was the only priest. I was saying nine Masses every Sunday. I had seven battalions, with about 3,000 men each, so a total of about 21,000 men, and at least one-third were Catholic. And you would say Mass one place and then have to fly somewhere else for another. You could never cover everyone.

I remember turning down one colonel who got really angry at me. I don't know how many Masses I had said, but god it was hot and I wasn't feeling well. He had flown in and he said to me, "Oh, I've been looking for a priest." It's Easter, and he wanted me to say a Mass. And I just couldn't. I was sick, had the flu. I had said maybe ten Masses and I hadn't eaten. I said, "Sir, I can't help it, I just can't. Pick me up tomorrow." And he was mad and turned around. But I would have fallen right on my face. I couldn't take one more step practically.

Typical Catholic Collection

Every week, we had to report the number of Masses we had, the number of people who attended, and we had to take up a collection, no matter where. That was all part of the process. My aid would take the collection and would turn it in to HQ. But I had seven guys working for me and it was really funny because I had a non-Catholic colonel working for me and he said, "Father, you're kind of cheating on your numbers. There are seven ministers and you're the only priest. You're having more attendance by yourself than these seven guys all put together, but your collections are way down." And I said, "But, sir, you don't know. The Catholic kids put in $.25, the Protestants put in $1.00 or $5.00, because that's what they're trained to do."

The Jeep Altar

When you fly into a war zone, you introduce yourself to the commanding officer. And he would explain where the troops are and then it's up to you to go out and take care of them. You had a kid, and he would be your aide or your driver and then you would go to the S-3 who would know what was happening, such as there's an artillery point here, and where the troops are and how to get to them. And it's up to you from then on. No one cares about you. You go ahead and take care of your job. There's no chapel or anything like that. You just said Mass wherever you could. On top of a Jeep even.

And then sleeping was another thing. You had a little mattress that you would blow up. I always put my mattress near where

the medics were or where the artillery
kids were, but mostly where the medics
were. You put your poncho down and you
hope it doesn't rain. If it rains,
sometimes you wake up and you're
floating.

Imagine, nighttime, no lights, and you're
sleeping under the bushes, and it's scary
as hell. Any noise you hear, boy, you're
wondering, "Oh geez." People don't
realize what soldiers go through.

The Welcome Reward

On the way to Vietnam, we got on the
plane from Travis to go to the war and,
boy, it's dark and cold, and everybody's
sitting there kind of quiet. I look back
and about two rows back there's another
major, and I was a major but with two
crosses. So I say to the kid next to me,
"Hey, there's another chaplain back
there. Would you mind changing seats?" So
this chaplain and I sit next to each
other. He was an Episcopal padre, an
Anglican, and he says to me, "So, are you
Roman Catholic?" And I said, "Yeah, I'm
Roman Catholic." And he said, "Do you
drink?" And I said, "I told you. I'm a
Roman Catholic priest." So he pulls out
this thermos of martinis that his wife
had made for him. So we're sitting there
sipping on martinis, flying off to war.
It was funny.

We talked and he said that we were both
stationed in the same division, the 1st

Division. We ended up seeing each other 7:00 every Sunday night. We would have our assistants barbecue for us. We would go to the sergeants and say, "Hey, you got any steaks tonight?" And they would say, "Oh, sure, Father," and give us some steaks. And we would barbecue and have a few shots. But I deserved it after saying nine Masses on Sunday.

The Not-So-Welcome Bunker Mate

Whenever you got mortared, you would dive into a bunker that was dug in the ground, and so this one time we were getting mortared and I dove into this bunker, and the next thing I see is this big snake. So I go outside and lie on the ground. I'm lying on my back and stuff is falling all over me. But I wouldn't go back into that bunker for the life of me. But I made it through alive.

Getting Shot At

In Korea, you were in trenches so you were stable. But in Vietnam, we were here or there and everywhere, so the only way to get places was by helicopter. Once, flying over Cambodia, I was riding with this pilot, a kid named Danny Walsh. He was a warrant officer, and we've got our earphones on because it was the only way you could hear. We could see these shots coming up from the jungle, shootin' at us, and one comes right through my legs with a BOOM. I looked down and there was one bullet hole right between my feet, right through the chopper. So Danny asks me through the earphones, "Are you scared Father?" I said, "No, Danny, but I just wet my pants." In those days we flew with two tanks of gas, and if one bullet had hit one of those…BOOM…crispy critters!

So I got shot at, but I was never wounded.

The Booming Mortars
In Vietnam there was this Captain, a West Pointer. And after one Viet Cong ambush he had eleven kids killed in his unit and he was all broken up. The colonel called me and said, "Father, I want you to go out there and take care of the Captain. We love him and he's a nice soldier, but he's all broken up." So I go out there and you see these kids, and they're all covered up, and all you see is their boots. So I took the Captain out by the wire because I didn't want him to break down in front of the kids. He was a good boy, a Catholic boy, and I said to him, "Now you've done your best. It wasn't your fault those kids were ambushed," and so forth. And while we're talking—BOOM—we started getting mortared. BANG, BANG. And I said, "Well, I'm getting out of here." We go back to the central point, the headquarters, and there's a slip trench there, and when you get mortared you just drop in there, fall into it for protection.

The Disappearing Trench

I decided: they're going to hit us again tonight so I'm going to have my bed here, so that when the mortars come, I just roll over and fall into this ditch. At about three in the morning, BOOM BOOM, the mortars start coming in. Instead of rolling toward the ditch, I turned the other way and couldn't find it, and I say, "Where's that f*ing trench?" and I bang my knee right into this kid's head and put it into the mud, and he turns to me and says, "You found the f*ing trench." Well, that story got around, and in fact the general came the next day and he asks, "Are you the chaplain that fell in the f*ing trench?" It went around to the whole outfit.

But you can't help it. When those mortars come BOOM, and you're walking ten yards or so, and they just keep coming closer and closer. It's terrifying. You jump into that pit. The overhead stuff that comes in, the artillery, it's all the same. It's death coming at you—BOOM BOOM BOOM. You're either in the wrong place at the wrong time or the right place at the right time.

The Tragedy of Dope

Another thing that happened to me: I got woken up one night by the lieutenant and he said, "We've got a situation down there. Three soldiers were in a hut waiting to go home, and this one guy stabbed one of them, and he's holding the

other one with a bayonet at the guy's
neck. Would you go in there and try to
talk them out of there?"

So I went in there. They were all black
kids. And this guy had a bayonet in his
hand. And I looked down on the floor and
I said, "That kid down there is dead."
And the kid with the knife said, "I know.
I know because I stuck him." And I said,
"Well, you're making it worse. Why don't
you give me that bayonet and get out of
here. You're going to be in trouble but
why make it worse than it is?" He said,
"No, no." I said, "Listen, if you trust
me, I'll go outside, the MPs will take
you and put you in the brig. But this kid
is dead and we have to do something about
that." The other poor kid, his eyes are
like this. So I went out to the MPs and
said, "He's ready to come out, but I
promised that you guys would take care of
him."

So the guy comes out and he has the
bayonet at the other kid's head. But as
he walks out the door the two MPs hit him
on the head with the billy clubs and he
went down like a rock. I don't know if he
was dead or not, but they took him out.
The poor kid with the knife. It was all
about dope, you see. Vietnam was worse
than Korea.

The Orphanage and the Leper Colony
So many little kids lost their parents.
These nuns had an orphanage somewhere

near our area. And I would go down once a week or so and bring them some food and candy. I would go over and fill my fatigues with candy and gum and stuff. When the little kids saw me they would run over and jump on me and take the candy. That was really a delight. And these Catholic nuns were Vietnamese, Korean, English, but they were good to us and they took care of us and these little kids and babies. We'd take stuff to the village, too. We weren't just fighting. We were trying to help people, too.

There was also a leper colony. And my colonel was very generous with it. He liked the priest over there who was running it, Father Victor Burset. Father Burset went around gathering the lepers, and he started a whole community. Our colonel was very good. He was a pilot. And the only way you could get out there to the colony was to fly. So about every week I would go out there, and I always brought Father Burset a bottle of bourbon. And that was all the poor guy had. It was terrible. We would fly over there and bring some relief.

I wrote here to Nativity to Claire Delaney, who was a nurse at Sequoia. And I said to her that I was at a leper colony, and that if they only had an X-ray machine they could do so much more, especially for the little kids. So she got together with some other doctors at Sequoia, and they got a used X-ray machine from Sequoia and sent it overseas and gave it to the leper colony. It was a wonderful gift.

One day Father Burset said to me, "You come with me. We're going to go through the wards." And I'm chicken because I'm thinking that I'm going to get this stuff. And he says, "Now, Father, come with me, they want to be touched." And he made me touch them and they would respond, "Ohh…." And we would read the scriptures, and they wanted to be touched. He made me touch them.

After the war, the Communists hung him. They hung him and they stole all the medicine and raped the nuns. They were Communists. Anything that was good for the people had to be eradicated.

The Village Tet Celebration

Also there was a little village. And the entire village had come from the north to the south for their faith. And there was this Father Lee, I think was his name. And he asked me to come down and say Mass with him. It was a big celebration, right around Tet, the Vietnamese New Year. So I came down and said Mass and started out, "In the name of the Father…" And they began to sing in Latin. They sang the whole thing in Latin. Yeah, they did.

We had a big banquet after. Now I'm very picky about what I eat. They had shrimp and there's no refrigeration and you see flies all over it. And so I just avoided it. There was another padre who came down, too, and he said, "Eat this stuff, it's really good." And I said, "Oh, no thank you." Imagine. I got a bottle of Orange Crush and sipped that and said, "I'm fine, I'm fine." That night that poor guy was out in the field throwing up. Sick as a dog.

Then, during Tet, the Communists came down and blew up that whole little village. Those people had come up out of the north for their faith. And the Communists didn't like that, so BOOM BOOM BOOM.

Chaplain Reports, Sending One Home
As brigade chaplain I had to write reports about each of my chaplains. I had to write about seven. There was this one guy, a Methodist. He was a nice young kid. And he wanted to stay in the Army. But we were being attacked this one time and instead of being with the kids, he went into hiding and wouldn't come out. And so afterwards the commander said to me, "Hey, Father, that chaplain didn't do very good and the kids know he was hiding." So I went over to talk to him and he said, "Well, I'm married and I have kids and I was scared." And I said, "Those other kids, they're married, and they have kids, and they're scared, too, but they don't hide. They have to stay and fight." And he started to cry. And so I gave him $200 and I went over to the

sergeant major and I said, "He's going on R&R to Japan." And so he went on R&R and he came back and he was better. But I had to write his efficiency report and so I wrote that he was a good chaplain and all that, but not recommended as combat chaplain.

Well, he was the chaplain to my commander, also a Methodist. And the commander called me in and he had my report there and he said, "Do you know that your report will keep him from being in the service?" And I said, "Yes, I know that it will." And he said, "Do you know that he's my chaplain?" And I said, "Yes, I do." And he said, "Do you know that I write your report?" And I said, "Yes, I do." And he said, "Are you still going to keep that?" And, I said, "Yes, sir, I am." So when my commander went through, he gave me a glowing report. Well, he knew I was right. The guy was no good in the sense that he didn't serve that purpose.

I was afraid, too, but you don't go into hiding. The kids can't. That was kind of a sad thing about that chaplain. But the rest of the chaplains were great. Every one of them. At some point or another, they would come to see me and I would act as their father confessor. If they were having problems with their wives or their kids or things like that. Every one of them. That's why most commanding officers always wanted a Catholic priest.

Vietnamese Devotion to the Mass

There was a whole battalion across in Thailand. Remember, we didn't even realize we had military in Thailand. There was a whole battalion of engineers there. They had built this little chapel, but there was no Catholic priest there. I was already saying nine Masses on Sunday, but I said, "If you get me a chopper and you get me out there, I will go out there on Sunday." So he did get the chopper and I went out there and said Mass. The last two pews in this little chapel they built were for Vietnamese, the people who worked around the headquarters. They came to Mass but they never went to Communion. So I got the head honcho and I asked, "You come to Mass, but why don't you go to Holy Communion?" "Oh Father," he says, "this is our Mass of Thanksgiving. We went to Mass at five this morning." They would walk five miles to work, go to a Mass of Thanksgiving, and then walk five miles back! Now would any of our people do that?

Language Problems

I was flying with my colonel one time and we were in a fire fight and you have your earphones in and you're listening to everyone and the bullets are coming in. And the colonel says, "Those goddam sons of bitches." Get 'em, you know. And he was using Jesus' name, and all of a sudden he says, "Geez, Father, I guess I've been using some bad language." And I said, "Sir, for a little man, you're throwing a big man's name around very carelessly." And all the other pilots suddenly got quiet. Finally we come back and the next day at staff meeting, the colonel says, "By the way, one other thing. I've noticed lately that there's a lot of bad language being used. Goddamit, I want it stopped." And, I went up to him afterwards and I said, "Well, sir, you really tried."

The Brothel that Never Was

The war was winding down, and the commanding officer made a decision that he was going to set up a brothel on the campgrounds. And so the XO said, "Hey, Father, you're not going to like this, but you should know that the colonel is going to set up a brothel. He said he's going to have the kids serviced. And I said, "Oh, okay." So I went over to the colonel and I knocked on his door and he said, "Oh, Father, come in." And I said, "Sir, I don't' know if this is right or not but I understand that there's a possibility that you might set up a Miss May's to service the kids." And he said, "Oh, Father, you just don't understand men…" and all that stuff. And I said, "Sir, I may not be able to stop it, but the moment one of their feet is standing on this ground I'm going to the general." And his eyes got big. He knew he couldn't do that. So I left and he didn't do it. But the XO said, "Hey, Father, what did you do?" And I said, "I just told him that if he did that, then I was going to go to the general. And so he tore the papers up. That's all he could do."

Hittin' the Chips
One time I was down in Saigon and we had a big, big PX down in Saigon. Man, they had everything. Well, there was a wedge [golf club], brand new. So I bought that wedge and I came back. I got one of the guys, who was the engineer, to cut a plank into little squares. So I put them behind my chapel and I would practice hittin' those little wood chips. So this one day I was out there hittin' the wood chips: I look up and hear the putt-putt of the colonel's helicopter. But then it went around and around and then it went back to his helipad. I saw him get out and he started walking. I thought, "Oh geez, he is coming right over to see me." He says, "Father was that you I saw? What were you doing?" I said, "I was practicing my wedge shot."

The War Goes on in Sickness and in Health
The water department of Saigon was a little bit outside the city. And we had this whole battalion of infantry out there protecting it because the Communists were trying to blow it up, to cut off the water to Saigon. I would go out there every week and say a couple of Masses because there were several hundred kids there. This one night, I'm down there and it's getting close to evening and my colonel flies in and he says, "Father, what are you doing down here?"

And I said, "I'm saying Mass for the
soldiers, sir." And he said, "Well, the
word is that we're probably going to get
hit tonight. We'll fly you out of here."
And I said, "Well, if they're going to
get hit, then I'm going to stay here. The
kids may need me." So he said, "Okay."
And so I said Mass, and as a matter of
fact the doctor served my Mass. And then
I ate chow.

It was about to get dark and so I put out
my bedroll near the medics, and then all
of a sudden I started to get real sick to
my stomach. Both ways. About five times.
And there's no place, no convenience. So
finally I went to the doctor and he said
to me, "Oh, my god. You're dehydrated.
I'm going to fly you to the hospital."
And I said, "No, no, they're going to
attack us tonight. I've got to be here."
So he gave me an IV and put me in a
stretcher.

Later, sure enough, there was a hit.
Machine guns were firing. And I'm
anointing kids and throwing up. Finally
the firing stopped. The doctor had his
fingers blown off, so they flew him out.
The next day I had to go back to HQ and I
got a ride from an ambulance. I opened up
a can of Coke at 8:00 a.m. and I sipped
it and sipped it until 4 p.m. to get one
can of Coke down me.

The next day was Sunday and I said nine
Masses.

You look back and you wonder how you did those things.

Korea and Vietnam Service Medals
I spent two years in Korea and five years in Vietnam. And of those five years of time, most of it was spent at the front lines. I think I got 12 medals. One of them [Commendation for Bravery under Extreme Battle Conditions] was during Tet. The Communists were all over. They were coming up and we were shooting them down like flies. But it also meant that we had a lot of our kids hit too. We had ambulances to take them to the big Army hospital they had there. But I also tried to get some of the kids who were wounded, and I just picked them up and put them in my Jeep and drove them to the hospital. In the meantime they are shooting at you. This was outside a place called Cho Lan.

"Father Lucky".

Chapter 9

Return from Vietnam

Fort Ord: Sticking the Dagger

When I got back from Vietnam, I was
chaplain for a while at Fort Ord. And I
had to make sure that the chaplains took
care of the convicts in the brig, where
there would be murderers, rapists,
everything. But I made sure that every
Sunday I said early Mass for the convicts
down there. And I also made my ministers
go there, so that every day there would
be a minister down there for the kids.
But I got a call this one day from the
commanding general and he said, "Father,
there's a big protest coming to the fort,
and they're saying that our chaplains are
not taking care of the prisoners. I want
you to go as my representative, and I'm
having the MPs escort these guys to your
chapel up there and you be my spokesman."
So I said, "Okay." Well, I had this
plaque in the office that the pilots, who
were good friends, had given me in
Vietnam. They put a dagger in this plaque
because my number was dagger one niner.
When I was out in the boonies I would
radio, "This is dagger one niner, come

pick me up." And the pilots would come pick me up. And then they got together and gave me this plaque. And I really cherished that.

Well I had put this plaque in my office at Fort Ord and this big protest came. There were all these people. There was a Franciscan priest and there was a nun and there was a Lutheran minister. So they all come to my office complaining about us not taking care of the prisoners. And I said, "I don't know where you all are on Sunday at five, but I'm down there saying Mass for the Catholic kids." Finally, this Lutheran minister looks up and he sees this dagger. And he says, "Is that a dagger on your wall?" And I said, "Yeah." And he says, "That's a symbol of violence." And I said, "Yeah, and right now I know where I would like to stick it." Well, that broke them up and they left.

The general called and I told him that and he got the biggest kick out of that. I still have that plaque in my room. It's falling apart.

Turning Down a VIP Job

I was in the reserves at the time and there was an opening for brigadier general chaplain back at the Pentagon. And the 6th Army chaplain on active duty called me and he said, "Art, you would be well qualified for that post and we would make sure you got it. We'd make you a brigadier general, but you would have to promise four years at the Pentagon." I said, "I don't want to be sitting behind a desk for four years," and said, "No, thank you." I turned it down because I'd be sitting in an office and I wouldn't have any contact with soldiers. I'd just be an administrator. And I wanted to be with people.

Military Service Ends: The Unwelcoming Parish Council

When I got out of the service I went home to my mother and she said, "The chancery called and they want to see you as soon as you get home." So I went up to the chancery and Archbishop McGucken tells me how I'd done this and done that and I'd done a good job. And so he says, "I have a problem in Pacifica. The priest there is leaving and he has been married and it's been causing quite the scandal. And I want you to go there and be at that parish." And I said, "Oh." But I went.

So one week after I left the service, I got assigned to St. Peter's in Pacifica. I took the place of a priest who was married for five years and had a child there. And half the parish knew about it. No other priest would go there because they knew what was up. It was a sad, sad place. The first parish council meeting I went to, there were 15 on the council and the chairman said, "Father we want to let you know that we have voted 9 to 6 not to accept you as our pastor." And I said,

"Why?" "Well, you were in the service and you wouldn't know anything about the needs of children or anything like that." So I said to him, "Well, the first thing I'm going to do is veto your vote."

In about a year's time things kind of calmed down. It was a beautiful parish, actually.

Return to Nativity

In 1976, my term as associate at St. Peter's was ending, and I got another call from the chancery. It was Archbishop McGucken. I said, "How are you? What's up?" He said, "You've done me two favors, and I appreciate it. What can I do for you?" And I said, "Well, I've always loved Nativity." He said, "Father Ford is there, but he's very sick." And I said, "Well, we're friends." And he said, "Well, if you're friends and he says it's okay, I'll make you the pastor over there tomorrow."

A gathering with my parents and brothers.
From left to right: My mother, me, Walter (my younger brother),
my father, and Bill.

Chapter 10

Church of the Nativity

Frank O'Hare

Frank O'Hare was a very charismatic person. I remember Frank used to come to the Tuesday evening Mass, and he would come up to my room and we would have a drink together and talk about things. And Sally would be looking for him and the phone would ring. Frank would be sitting over there having a drink and someone would say, "Oh, hi, Sally." And she would say, "Have you seen Frank?" Frank would be waving his hand no. And I would say, "Yeah, I ran into Frank awhile ago." I didn't lie.

One day—it was a hot day—and I think I was going over to church to hear confessions and Frank runs over waving his hands. I said, "Geez, Frank. What are you doing here?" And he says, "Father, you have your golf and I have Nativity." Frank just loved Nativity. He was just 56 when he got hit by a motorcyclist.

Nuns' Stories

In the early days at Nativity I used to say Mass over there at the monastery every day at 6:45. Sunday, Christmas, Easter, whatever. It was a duty of this parish that the assistant or pastor would say Mass for the nuns. But one day the Mag (Father Magner) called me and he said, "Well, Art, you don't have to worry about the Dominicans anymore." And I said, "Why?" And he said, "Because I'm retiring and going over there and I'll be taking over the Mass there." But then he started getting sick and so the nuns would still call me every once in awhile. This one time I went over there with the Oil of the Sick and he was lying on the floor, all vested. I looked down with the oil and he said, "Hi, Art, what are you doing?" and I said, "I'm going to anoint you." And, he said, "Well, go ahead." He was my professor at the seminary. He told taught us the sacraments. Terrific guy. One eye. We called him Cyclops.

The best thing for me was when I was the quasi-chaplain for the Dominicans and they had their election to vote in their Mother Superior. There had to be three priests, so there was myself and Father Mohr for a while, and we got Monsignor Kennedy for a while, so there were three priests. So the nuns were praying and filling out ballots and they all wrote the names down as who they wanted as their prioress. So, I was taking the ballots and reading out, "Sister Mary of This, That and the Other," "Sister Mary from Behind the Rock," "Sister Mary Who Doesn't Know Her Nose," and then I read off "Jimmy Carter." They all broke up.

Bill Zappettini
I have a good story about Bill and myself. We were down in Palm Springs, a lovely place. We had a golf game scheduled down in Thunderbird at 11:00 or so. It was around Mother's Day, and Bill said to me that he had all kinds of roses at his hothouse, and he said, "Would you like to see them?" And I said, "Sure I would." So we got into the car. It was Paula's mother's car. And we drove down there, and all of a sudden we needed to make a left turn. And, I said, "Bill, it looks pretty sandy." So the wheels are spinning and we're stuck in the sand. We both get out of the car. And Bill goes walking off and I go to this place and flag down a truck and explain what happened. So Bill comes back and we put a rope on the car, and the truck driver pulls us out and off we go. And Bill says, "Father, what did you do?" And I said, "Well, I was trying to get a car to pull us out. What were you doing?" And he said, "I was praying."

Jack Hollywood
Jack Hollywood was the fire marshal, and he was the athletic director here at Nativity. He was a good guy and he had leukemia. He went very quickly. He came to see me one week before he died and he said, "Father, they told me I only had a couple of weeks." And they were right. He didn't last long. Afterward, Frank O'Hare

asked me to come out and do a special
blessing in between those two redwood
trees in honor of Jack Hollywood. And I
said, "Sure." Those trees are huge now.

Emily, The Four-Year-Old Judge
One of the nuns who had taught class here
died, and I was brought in to say the
funeral Mass. After the Mass we get in
the car and go to the cemetery. Then
four-year-old Emily gets out and she runs
ahead right in front of me. So we're
there at the coffin and grave and I just
let her stay standing there in front.
Some of the nuns toss some dirt into the
grave, and Emily picks up some dirt and
throws some in, too. I say some final
prayers and she looks at me and she says,
"Good job, Father."

Emily's parents, Amy and Richard, one
time had their house broken into during
the workday. The burglars took TVs and
some computers and stuff. They really got
hit. While we were going up to the nun's
funeral, Emily asks Bonnie, "Uh, Grandma,
why doesn't Father Davenport have a wife?
Why isn't he married?" And so Bonnie said
to me, "You explain it to her." So I
tried to explain it to her. "Well, we
priests try to do what we can for people
when they need us. We're there. But if
you have a family you have to take care
of your family first and stuff." Emily
looks at me and says, "Well, you didn't
do any good for me when my house was

burglarized!" Four years old!

I always wanted to be a parish priest.
This is me with a baby I baptized.

Giants and 49ers: Root, Root, Root for the Home Team!

I root for the Giants, but I'm not really particular about them. I don't go to games. The 49ers, I've been going to their games since they were instituted in 1948 when I was ordained. And I got season tickets from the time I was ordained till now. So you could say I've had an interest. And the Policys were members of the parish. They were the general managers of the 49ers. Mrs. Policy came to Mass almost every day here, and we became great friends. They even took me back to Washington D.C. with the players when they were going to play football back there, and it was terrific. I had a real close association with them.

Mother Costello would come over and I used to tease her and say, "Mother you've got to pray for the 49ers." Well, I was kidding her. But a lot of people thought that I meant it.

Chapter 11

Golf Stories

Playing with Fellow Priests

I got started with golf in the seminary.
A lot of us, when we got to major
seminary, had Thursday off, and we would
get one of the professors to take us up
to Crystal Springs and play golf. So
that's how I started playing. And then
afterwards it was just with classmates,
or priest friends, and on vacations with
priests who played golf. The best score I
ever had anywhere was 66, at Bonnie's
course at Pacific Grove, which is a very
small little course. It's beautiful. The
backside of the course is just beautiful.

Do you remember Father Jim Mohr? Well,
Jim was playing us one day and he was all
nervous. We got to the first hole and he
probably had 8 or 9 shots. Then the next
hole he shot went down a big ravine, and
finally he is up and maybe he's 100 yards
from the green. He already had about 10
shots and he's very nervous, and he said
to the caddy, "What should I use?" The
caddy handed him a club, and the other

caddy said, "A driver, if I know anything." Poor Jim.

Getting the Swing Back

When I came back from Korea, the guys I had been playing with had gotten much better while I was gone. So I decided: I've got to get some lessons if I'm going to play with these guys. So I see this sign on the driving range that said "Willy Nichols." I went to Mr. Nichols and said, "I'm a priest. I just got out of the service and I would like to take some lessons." And he said, "Oh no, Father, some of those pros come back to me. I'm retired." And I said, "Well, just talking to you was an honor." So he says, "Well, let me see you swing." So I swung, and he said, "Father, do you like to suffer? I'll give you a lesson, provided you do one thing. No matter how poorly you play, you just keep trying to do what I tell you to do." So I said, "Okay." And I took lessons. And then six months later I was shooting in the 70s.

This one Sunday, I went out to hit balls at Bay Meadows. He was out there, and Johnny Culligan was playing in the masters championship. It's a huge, big tournament. And Willy had taught him since he was a little kid. But he was having a real hard time with his three wood. So Willy says, "Father, go out there and get some balls and take out your three wood." So I did. He said, "Tommy, watch the Father." So I start hitting some balls, and the balls were going whew-whew! And he said, "Father, if you were a woman I would make love to you." I was playing really well. I shot an 80. I beat the pro by 5 shots. There was some visiting general, too. The kids put it in the newspaper: "Chaplain burns up course. Chaplain burns up General." Willy was great. Before he died I went out to see him at the hospital. He was Presbyterian, but a real respectful Scotsman.

Walking and Talking with Lee Trevino

While I was at Fort Ord, there was the annual Pebble Beach Golf Tournament. They announced there was going to be an exhibition game with Lee Trevino, Dave Stockton, and two other golfers. So a lot of people turned out, and I come out in my fatigues and I'm standing behind the reps, and Trevino is looking over at me and motioning like this. So I'm looking over, and then he goes like this again. So finally I go over to him. He had recognized the two crosses, and so he says to me, "Are you a priest?" And I said, "Yeah." And he said, "Father, walk with me." So here we are, and he's talking all the way during the game. "Now Father, some of the guys are real quiet, but I have to talk like this or else I would go crazy." I'll never forget it. And he made one of the toughest shots. You have to fly a ball over the trees and then turn left. And he did a real great job. A 79 hitter. And some lady started jumping all around and clapping and he said, "Lady, what are you clapping for? I'm the national champion. I should be hitting the ball like that." He was terrific.

The Tuesday Morning Group

So what can I say about the Tuesday morning group that we've been playing golf with for over 20 years? It's partly why I'm still a priest. It may sound ridiculous, but it's partly true. I was telling Father Roland the same thing. I said, "Roland, on your day off, I want you to start playing golf. You'll be with other priests. You'll be doing things to keep yourself being a good priest." And it may sound ridiculous, but otherwise what does a priest do on his day off? Well, if he doesn't have something to do, then he thinks that maybe he has to have something.

When I first started playing with John Conway, that's when I had my first heart attack. I didn't even know that John played golf. And, I just mentioned to him that I would like to meet someone to play with and he said, "I'll play with you." We played the Ocean Course. And I mentioned to John how good it would be to play at the Olympic Club, and he said, "Well, I know a member who can get you on." And it was Art Sullivan. And we met Art that day up there and John introduced me. And I said to Art that I would love to play. So we met that next Tuesday and

he had us signed up at the Olympic Club
and we went up and played by the lake.
And now we've been playing for over 20
years. We picked up Father Gaffey along
the way and Father O'Connell. And boy, as
priests when we go away we stay at John's
place in Palm Desert.

Priests on the green. Left to right: A lay friend of Fr. Warner, myself, Fr. John Dollard, and Fr. William Warner.

Chapter 12

Lourdes

The Presence of Mary...of Peace...of Calm
Monsignor Otellini got to talking and he says, "You know, I think you would be a good candidate to go to Lourdes as a *malade*." You know, because of my heart and so forth. And I said "Oh, I'd be happy to!" So I was assigned, and we flew to Paris with the Zappettinis. This was 2006. We spent two days in Paris, then we took the train to Lourdes. As soon as we got there I went down to the grounds where there is this magnificent big cathedral, and underground there is one that is bigger. It is hard to believe. You have to see it.

I felt the presence of Mary, so powerful, so powerful! Now I am not a religious nut, but in fact we were saying Mass right in the grotto where the Blessed Mother appeared. A couple hundred priests, some bishops, two cardinals. Twice during the Mass I turned around because I thought someone was standing right behind me. I know it sounds nutty. I felt the presence of Mary so very, very close. How do you explain it? I don't know. Emotionally, probably, but nevertheless I just had that feeling about the love of Mary and how she leads to Jesus. For me, I've always loved the Mother of God, but this made it a really personal kind of thing.

When you get there you are assigned to a different color. There is red, blue, green—different colors. Groups, they call them. Whenever you went down to the grotto you had to be pushed if you were a *malade*. When I went down the stairs there was this young girl, I guess a college girl, and I could pick her up with one hand. And here she was going to be pushing me in the wheelchair. And I said "No, no—I will push you!" Well, the tears started to come down her face. Then she says "Oh, Father. I came here. I want to do something to help the sick." I said "Ohhh." And I got in and said, "Go ahead," and went on. From then on, no problem.

But there was another thing. There were a lot of places for confession. I asked Monsignor if I, as a *malade*, could hear confessions. He said, "I think I can arrange it for you." So he did. He just got the head guy over there and I would hear confessions in English. And there is this big building set apart just for confessions—American, Polish, German, Italian—all kinds. I had the English one. There happened to be a group of kids from the University of Michigan doing a pilgrimage. So it was their day to go to confession. They were all English speakers so they lined up. The door opened and this one girl came in. I had my stole on and she started, "No, no, Father, I don't believe in that stuff anymore. I just came in here because I didn't want my fellow classmates know that I don't believe in that stuff anymore." I said "Oh that's fine, just sit down and we will talk for a while." And we started talking. I said "So you are a university student. Do you learn something there?" She says "Oh yeah, Father, I go to that university now and they've got powerful teachers and so on." But I said, "That's great, but I don't think there is any more powerful teacher then Jesus." I looked at her and then I noticed little tears coming down there. But then I got scared. I got to talking to her and—wow—everything came out. She made a beautiful confession. In fact the next day, when she came to Mass, I was in a wheelchair and she saw me. "Oh Father, Father, I am so happy!" So it is hard to explain. It is an experience.

Then you go to a place that is set apart and there is the river. They diverted a part of the river that goes right down. That's the bath that you go into. They curtained it off. The bath is about as large as my room here. You go one at a time there, male and female—they are separated of course. You strip everything off and you go into the baths. There are two men beside you, they're volunteers.

They come from all over. They hold you
and then they ask you, "Do you want to be
immersed?" I said, "Yes." Down they go.
And they shove you under the water and
then pull you back up. Then they ask you,
"Would you like water to drink?" I said
"Yes." They take a cup out of there. You
drink that water—it's sacred water. And
then you get out. The first thing I said
was, "Well, where is the towel?" There is
no towel. You just put your clothes back
on and you are dry. I am not kidding you.
You know, if you are taking a shower and
afterward you'd be putting on your T-
shirt it would be clinging to you. It is
hard to believe. But there was a non-
Catholic fellow just ahead of me who went
to the baths. The same thing happened to
him. He said to me, "Father, I have to do
some powerful thinking." You know it is
for everybody, but the *malades* they treat
differently. There is an aura about it.

Once you are there, you sense an awful
lot of peace in people. And all the
people right there they say, "Hey, I
didn't come here primarily for a cure,
but I came here to be closer to Jesus."
And that happens. It happened to me, I
must say. There is calmness and a
peacefulness about your life. You just
recognize it. You know Mary is walking
with you. And there are so many things
that happen there. Every Friday night
there is a procession and you recite the
rosary. And then at the end of each
decade they sing, "Ave, Ave." We had

15,000 people that night at the
procession. It is hard to believe. And at
Mass in the lower cathedral 25,000
people. It just blows your mind. But
Monsignor told me that of all the shrines
in the world that's the most attended: 7
million people a year. Little less than a
million go to Mecca every year.

Chapter 13

Sixty Years a Priest

My thing is that I always wanted to be a parish priest. I wanted to be with people, and God has helped me do that in so many ways. By being in the Army I certainly was with people, being in the hospital I was with people, being in a parish I am with people. I feel that God has been good to me. More than 60 years in the priesthood. I've always been with people. That's all I always wanted to do.

My Life

I have had a great life. God is good. And as you are getting older you just feel the presence of Jesus and Blessed Mother. I feel the closeness of Mary to me very often. And standing there and holding the Host I keep saying, "Wow, this is God's body!" I think the older you get the more you become aware of it. When I was younger—you know you say all the prayers—but I think that as you grow older as a priest there is this union with Jesus. I wonder why he has kept me so long. After 87 years I am pretty much looking forward to seeing Jesus. It just blows your mind.

And Mary! My dad—he could visualize Mary.
When I was at the seminary, I would often
go home on Sunday and my dad and I would
stop and talk about a number of things.
On this one Sunday in particular—he was
very, very holy—he said to me, "Art, I
pray and pray and I try to think of God,
but God is so immense." And he said, "I
can't visualize God, but wouldn't it be
great if when we walk through the gates
the person we meet is Mary." He said,
"First time you see Mary, what a
wonderful thing that must be!" That's
something I am looking forward to.

I have seen a lot of pain and death in my
life. They ask me how I do it—after
having experienced all that—how I am
still smiling and being positive. Well,
that is what life is all about. That is
what God is all about. That is what Jesus
is all about. It is not just when things
are good. It is when the things are bad—
that's when He really shows Himself to
you.

See, as an Army chaplain you are all by
yourself most of the time and yet the
Blessed Sacrament is with you, and at
night time you go to the trenches. It's
30 below zero and you get in the sleeping
bag—all you could do is pray. What else
you could do at night when it gets dark?
You could listen for the footsteps of the
Chinese coming up after you. Well, I did
have Danny. We would have a bunk together
and we would talk. It's funny—he'd go,

"Are you asleep Father?" And I'd say, "No, Danny 'cause you keep talking."

But the presence of Jesus at Mass you feel—wow! At the consecration—and you think how unworthy you are, there are things you fouled up in your life and you think, "Oh, how could I do that?" Well, Jesus loves me. Jesus forgives me. And I understand that. So many people get afraid—"Oh, God can't forgive me." That's nonsense. I trust in Him. Boy, that Divine Mercy. That's the last thing I say when I go to bed. Put yourself in God's hands completely. Sister Faustina—I read her book. The message is quite simple: "Trust in Jesus!" So many people don't.

It has been a wonderful life. I am looking forward to go to heaven. It's out there. It's waiting for us.

.   .   .

Fr. Clement Arthur Davenport.
United States Army Colonel, Retired.

Made in the USA
San Bernardino, CA
31 August 2014